The Prophetic Book Abdias: The Destruction of Edom

Bible Sermons

Published by Seminit Publications, 2024.

THE PROPHETIC BOOK ABDIAS: THE DESTRUCTION OF EDOM

First edition. May 7, 2024.

Written by Bible Sermons.

Table of Contents

Nahum 2:13. *And I will burn their chariots in smoke, and the sword shall devour thy young lions; and I will cut off thy prey from the earth, and the voice of thy messengers shall be heard no more.*

It is high time they were stopped. You remember with what foul language Rabshakeh addressed King Hezekiah; and God now declares that there will be no more letters like his. God may allow evil to rule over his people for a time; but then he puts a hook in the leviathan's mouth. He that restraineth the sea and the waves thereof, Jehovah is his name, and restraineth the wickedness of men.

— **Charles Spurgeon**

Introduction

Obadiah's prophecy is much more practical and understandable than you might imagine. It is a pity that there are certain books in the Bible that we neglect. The Word of God teaches about itself on the clarity that its content possesses. This is what is commonly called the Perspicuity of Scripture. This doctrine teaches that the Bible is a clear, intelligible and understandable text. God has revealed His Word in this way because He has a deep passion to reveal His purposes to men with perfect clarity.

David said of God's Word, "The law of the LORD is perfect, converting the soul; the testimony of the LORD is faithful, making wise the simple" (Ps. 19:7). Paul describes the Scriptures as being useful (2 Tim. 3:16). Obadiah, and all the other books of the Bible, should not be seen as being nebulous and confusing writings. God inspired His Word in such a way that we can understand it; and He has also provided us with the Holy Spirit and teachers in the church to help us discern it.

In this very simple and brief booklet I try to convince you that Obadiah's prophecy is understandable, interesting and applicable. Before considering the prophecy, I want to suggest to you that there are at least four points that can be drawn out in this book that will make Obadiah very useful to you.

Theologically. The most important thing about every book in the canon of Scripture, including Obadiah's prophecy, is what we learn about God. Study Obadiah desiring to learn about

God's attributes. This prophecy teaches us about His sovereignty, faithfulness, righteousness, omnipotence. Obadiah makes us admire God's character more, which results in us worshipping Him more deeply.

2. Practical. There are very practical things in this book inspired by God that benefit us in our daily walk before the Lord. We learn that we can be like Obadiah, who although not much is known about him from what we read in the book that bears his name, he was faithful to the Lord and greatly pleased Him. We understand through this prophecy the importance of putting sin to death in us because of the severe consequences of perversion. We see this by analyzing the example of Edom.

3. Ecclesially. Obadiah is a book so applicable to our lives that it also guides us in our treatment of our brothers in Christ. It exhibits how horrendous it is for the Lord of glory when brethren are in discord and conflict. Obadiah's prophecy also exhibits how wrong we are when we do not do something about brethren who have spiritual needs, and worse yet, we make their situation more difficult by treating them unjustly.

4. Prophetically. This book we will be considering has a focus on prophetic themes. We seek to explain the meaning of the day of the LORD and how it fits into God's prophetic program. Obadiah's prophecy also makes it clear as to certain purposes he has for Israel in the future. The book concludes by making mention of the coming kingdom of the Lord, which we seek to explain by looking at the impact this should have on every Bible student.

May the Lord use this simple consideration of Obadiah to edify the saints (1 Cor. 14:26) and to exalt the One who one day in the future will reign over all the earth from Zion (Obad. 21).

1. The humiliation of Edom (v.1-4)

Vision of Obadiah. Thus saith the Lord GOD concerning Edom: We have heard the cry of the LORD, and a messenger is sent unto the nations. Arise, and let us rise up against this people in battle (v.1).

This Old Testament prophecy is a vision of Obadiah. The root of the word vision is related to "to look" and "to prophesy". This means that God manifested something to one of His servants and he communicated it to others. Not necessarily about events that would take place in the future, but in general they revealed the Word of God. Habakkuk was asked to write and declare the vision he received from the Lord (Hab. 2:2). The books of Isaiah and Nahum also begin in the manner in which the book of Obadiah begins (Isa. 1:1; Nah. 1:1). It seems common that these visions were received by night (Isa. 29:7).

God decided to reveal His purposes in different ways throughout the ages (Heb. 1:1). One of those ways was through visions, as He did during the times of the prophets. We should not think that this occurred constantly, for there were periods of time when visions were scarce (1 Sam. 3:1; Lam. 2:9; Ezek. 7:26; 12:22, 24). This was because of the unbelief of the nation of Israel. Solomon said, "Without prophecy [vision] the people run wild" (Prov. 29:18). As the canon of the Scriptures has been closed (Jud. 3), God does not communicate to us through visions as He did to His people through Obadiah. Today God speaks to us through His written Word. False prophets existed in

Old Testament times and abound today. Just because someone claims to have received a vision from God, that person should not be believed. In the times of the prophets there were those who falsely reported that God had given them vision (Jer. 14:14; 23:16; Ezek. 13:16). Today we also have to beware of people who do exactly the same thing.

There are more than a dozen men mentioned in the Bible with the same name as Obadiah, but apparently none of them is the same as the one mentioned in this prophecy. His name means: "servant of Jah [Jehovah]". His parents must have called him this name because of their desire for him to focus on service to God. The Lord in His sovereignty chose him for that very purpose. Obadiah was called by God to serve Him as His prophet. His name can also mean: "worshipper of Jah [Jehovah]". This also aptly summarizes his life. Obadiah was someone who sought to magnify the Lord through his life.

Obadiah is included in the list of minor prophets: Hosea to Malachi. They are not called minor prophets because they are less important than the major prophets. The major prophets are: Isaiah, Jeremiah, Ezekiel and Daniel. Obadiah and the other books in their category are called minor prophets because of their brevity. If we consider the books of the Bible written in their original language, Obadiah is the shortest book in the Old Testament, having only about 440 words. To put it in perspective, the book of Jeremiah contains about 33,000 words. Obadiah is the fourth shortest book in the entire Bible. It ranks after 3 John, 2 John and Philemon.

There are at least two factors about this book that might discourage us from reading, studying and teaching it. First, it is found in the Old Testament, which is the part of the Bible that is not taught as much as the New Testament. Second, because of its brevity, which might make us think that for that reason it does not have as much importance as other books do because they are longer. We must put into practice that we not only believe that all the Scriptures are inspired, but also that all the Word of God is useful to us (2 Tim. 3:16). We should be in the habit of reading, studying and teaching the gospel of John, the book of Numbers, the epistle of Jude and the prophecy of Obadiah. Every local church would be greatly blessed if every book of the Bible were taught verse by verse by men who are devoted to the study of the Word. Although Obadiah is never quoted in the New Testament, it is a book that is a blessing to all who search it. It is possible that we can find two allusions of this book in the New Testament: Obadiah 8 in 1 Corinthians 1:19 and Obadiah 21 in Revelation 11:15.

We are not given specific information about Obadiah's life other than that he received this vision from God. From what we read in this book, we can deduce that he prophesied to the southern kingdom and not to the northern kingdom, because Jerusalem and Judah are mentioned (v.11, 12, 17, 21). This is really the only thing we can know about this servant of God.

Neither can we be sure when Obadiah prophesied. One of the factors that distinguishes the prophets as to the time of their ministry is in relation to the exile that Israel suffered. On different occasions, Gentiles exiled the Lord's people to dwell in a foreign land. Some prophets prophesied before the exile as in the case of Hosea and Isaiah. Others prophesied during the exile, as did Ezekiel and Daniel. Others prophesied after the exile, as was the case of Haggai and Malachi. It seems from the content of Obadiah's prophecy that he prophesied before the exile and before the destruction of Jerusalem. When reading this book, the Holy Spirit gives us to understand that although the city had been attacked, it had not been completely annihilated, as it would be at the hand of the Babylonians. The similarities between this book and Jeremiah 49:7-22, prophesying the Babylonian invasion, could be a confirmation. Therefore, Obadiah possibly prophesied at the same time as Elijah and Elisha did.

Regarding these four attacks, the same author points out the following:

> Of these four, only the second and fourth fit the historical data. Number two is preferable, since Obadiah's description does not indicate the total and absolute destruction of the city, which took place under Nebuchadnezzar's attack. Moreover, although the Edomites were involved in Nebuchadnezzar's destruction of Jerusalem (Ps. 137; Lam. 4:21), it is significant that Obadiah does not mention the Babylonians by name (as with all the other prophets who wrote about the fall of Jerusalem), nor is there any reference to the destruction of the temple or the deportation of the people; in fact, the captives seem to have been taken southwest, not east of Babylon (v. 20).

Obadiah's prophecy begins by indicating what its main focus is . Jehovah the Lord has said this concerning Edom. Most prophets prophesied primarily to the nation of Israel, but others did the same to Gentile nations. Jonah and Nahum prophesied to Nineveh. Amos also foretold things to Edom as did Obadiah.

The inhabitants of Edom were descendants of Esau (Gen. 25:30; 36:1, 9), son of Isaac and twin brother of Jacob. Genesis 25 and 27 help us greatly to understand the background of the book of Obadiah. In these passages we read about what God anticipated about the descendants of these two characters before they were born and how this unfolded in their lives. Obadiah mentions the conflicts that the descendants of Esau and Jacob had. The antagonism between the two of them goes all the way back to when they were in the womb of their mother Rebekah. God announced to Isaac and Rebekah about the rivalry that would always exist between the descendants of their twin sons. All this would manifest itself when Esau sold his birthright to Jacob and when Jacob stripped Esau of his blessing by cheating his father Isaac.

The hatred between these two peoples reached the point that God's people would remind the Lord of Edom's desire to have Jerusalem destroyed. They said in Psalms 137:7, "O LORD, remember against the children of Edom the day of Jerusalem, when they said, 'Raze it, raze it to the ground.'" This is the central point of the prophecy under consideration. In Obadiah, the Lord details the fall of Edom for their sin and what they did against Jacob.

As we study the nation of Edom, it would be helpful to note a few other things about Esau, their father. The meaning of Esau's name, his occupation as a farmer and hunter, his favorite food, relates him to the color red and to the earth. This makes us see how Esau was an earthly man. He opposed spiritual truths, the people of God and the eternal kingdom of Jehovah.

Esau was a hairy man and the Edomites' Mount Seir means "hairy". Perhaps they have the same meaning because the topography of Seir was coarse sandstone. The meaning of his name, speaks of Esau's disorderly life. The idea behind him being related to abundance of hair is to resemble an animal. He lived, thought and behaved bestially. Hebrews 12:16 summarizes Esau's life in two ways. He is described as being a "fornicator" and "profane".

Esau disregarded the covenant God made with his fathers and departed from where they dwelt to marry women of Canaan and a daughter of Ishmael. Recall that Ishmael was born of an illicit relationship between Abraham and Hagar, who was an Egyptian handmaid of Sarah. Esau would settle in a mountainous region south of the Dead Sea, south of Judah and Moab, which would be called Edom or Idumea. The Edomites conquered the Horites who dwelt in that region (Gen. 36:8-43; Deut. 2:12, 22).

The rivalry between Esau and Jacob would endure even after they both died.

In Numbers 20 we read about how the Edomites would not allow the Israelites to pass through their land after they were redeemed by God from slavery in Egypt. Where the children of Edom settled, it was known as The Kings Highway, because it linked North Africa with Europe and Asia. In this book they will be condemned for not helping Israel, even though they were located in a strategic location, and had the means to help them. During the time of the kings, Edom would be subjugated by Israel during the reigns of David and Solomon (1 Sam. 14:47; 2 Sam. 8:14; 1 Kings 9:26). Some time later they would gain their freedom and again be dominated by Israel on at least two more occasions. On one occasion they allied with the Moabites to attack Judah but were defeated (2 Chron. 20:1-27). Edom would later be controlled by the Assyrians and Babylonians. Five hundred years before the birth of Jesus Christ they would be attacked by the Nabataeans, a tribe of Arabia and forced to leave their land. In 70 A.D., when the Romans attacked Jerusalem, the Edomites would try to join the Israelites to fight against them, but they would lose and thus disappear completely. We will see that God prophesied that this would happen through the prophet Obadiah (v.10, 18).

Another example of the rivalry between the seed of Edom and Jacob is what we see in the story of the birth of the Lord Jesus. King Herod, who was a descendant of Esau, wanted to kill Jesus Christ, who was a descendant of Jacob. This is one of the most recurring themes in the Bible. The Old Testament and the New Testament present to us what God anticipated when Adam sinned. "I will put enmity between you and the woman, and between your seed and her seed; she shall bruise your head, and you shall bruise her heel" (Gen. 3:15). The rivalry between the seed of the woman and the seed of the serpent is a key theme in understanding the Scriptures. The prophecy of Obadiah demonstrates how the seed of the woman, the Lord Jesus Christ, defeats the seed of the serpent, the devil.

Obadiah's prophecy presents us with the following five aspects about Edom:

Edom's humiliation (v.1-4) 2. Edom's destruction (v.5-9) 3. Edom's wickedness (v.10-14) 4. Edom's foreshadowing (v.15, 16) 5. Edom's rival (v.17-21)

The most important thing we can learn about Obadiah's prophecy is about the character of God. We should read and study all the books of the Bible wanting to know what they teach us about God. Each book of the Bible teaches us about the Person, attributes, works and purposes of the Lord. The prophet Obadiah presents to us far beyond what we can understand about God. Obadiah describes His faithfulness, righteousness, sovereignty, omnipotence, omniscience.

The prophet of the Lord said: We have heard the proclamation of the Lord. The word "proclamation" means "report", "news", "rumor". Obadiah had received a vision and a proclamation from God. This same word proclamation was used by other prophets. Isaiah asked the well-known question, "Who has believed our report?" (Isa. 53:1). The prophet Jeremiah spoke of a rumor that was to come (Jer. 10:22). Ezekiel warned that there would be "rumor upon rumor" concerning all that Judah would suffer (Ezek. 7:26). In Daniel 11:44 we read of "tidings." Obadiah is the only one of the prophets who begins his prophecy with this word.

In speaking about the rumor that Jehovah had shown him, Obadiah said: messenger has been sent to the nations. The prophet is presented as an envoy, ambassador and messenger of God who is sent to the nations in representation of Him. He was being sent to the nations to warn them of the fact that they would be attacked. The Hebrew word used by the Holy Spirit in speaking of the nations is typically used to refer to the Gentile peoples. In the case of Obadiah's prophecy, this word will be used when speaking of the nation of Edom (v.2) and all nations in general (v.15, 16). It is commonly perceived that the prophets of Israel only prophesied to their countrymen but Obadiah is a clear example that they also prophesied to the Gentile nations.

In this way Jehovah manifested His supremacy and sovereignty over Israel, but also over all the Gentile nations.

In Jeremiah 49:14 we read concerning this something very similar to what we read in Obadiah. "The tidings I heard, that a messenger was sent from the LORD unto the nations, saying, Gather yourselves together, and come against her, and go up to battle." As we study Obadiah, we should compare it with what we read in Jeremiah 49:7-22. The Spirit led Jeremiah to use Obadiah's prophecy in writing his prophecy. This also helps us to place Obadiah in the historical time in which he served God and the nation of Israel.

In summary, Obadiah's message to Edom is: Arise, and let us rise up against this people in battle. God commands His army to rise up against the Edomites to fight against them. The greatness of God's power and the awesomeness of His authority is seen in the fact that He repeats on two occasions that He will rise up against them. Armies will overthrow Edom, but it will all be the work of God who is in control of all things.

━━━◦━━━

Behold, I have made you small among the nations; you are greatly distressed (v.2).

The first thing God communicates about Edom is how He was punishing them for their sin by humiliating them. Despite the certain power they had enjoyed, the Lord God had made them small among the nations. He had made them insignificant and unimportant. He had also greatly cast them down. The dejection they had suffered had made them contemptible, vile, and worthless. The prophet Jeremiah said of them in this regard:

"Behold, I will make you small among the nations, despised among men" (Jer. 49:15).

They had enjoyed being well regarded because of the alliances they had made with strong nations, but now they were suffering the opposite as God's punishment. He humiliates those who try to exalt themselves above His Person and His purposes . "The wicked by the haughtiness of his countenance seeketh not God: there is no God in any of his thoughts. His ways are crooked at all times; Your judgments are far from his sight; all his adversaries he despises" (Ps. 10:4, 5).

———— ◉ ————

The pride of thy heart hath deceived thee, O thou that dwellest in the clefts of the rocks, in thy most high habitation; that sayest in thine heart, Who shall bring me down to the ground? (v.3)

In verses 10-14 we will see the wickedness of Edom, but here we are also made to see the pride of this nation. Not only had they been proud, but their pride had deceived their heart. They would deceive themselves by their vanity and would also be deceived by their allies (v.7). Pride is at the root of all sins. Pride blinds the wicked and also the children of God. It does not let them see how bad they are and how much they sin against the God of heaven. Solomon warns, "Pride goeth before destruction, and haughtiness of spirit before a fall" (Prov. 16:18). He also taught against arrogance when he wrote, "Every one that is haughty in heart is an abomination to the LORD; he shall not be unpunished" (Prov. 16:5).

God compares Edom's arrogance to an eagle that dwells on the heights of a rock. They thought they could never be brought down from their lofty dwelling. They thought they could hide themselves like the dove that hides "in the holes of the rock, in the covert of the steep places" (Can. 2:14). The great city of Petra was located in an extremely inaccessible place. Its height and surroundings protected them from their enemies. This made them feel completely invincible. It was not a rich and great nation as other nations were, but they did boast of the geographical location they had.

> Petra, the imposing and impregnable capital city of Edom, which lived in difficult mountainous terrain, was virtually inaccessible, giving it a sense of security and self-sufficiency. Deep, terrifying gorges emanating from peaks reaching 5,700 feet [1,737 meters] surrounded it like a fortress, generating a proud, false sense of security.

Jeremiah also commented concerning this. "Your arrogance has deceived you, and the pride of your heart. You that dwell in caves of rocks, that have the height of the mountain, though you lift up your nest like an eagle, from there will I bring you down, says the LORD" (Jer. 49:16). No one had been able to bring them down, but God would do it without any difficulty. God would be like an eagle far mightier than the eagle of Edom to overcome them. "Behold, he shall mount up as an eagle, and fly, and spread his wings over Bozrah: and the heart of the mighty men of Edom shall be in that day as the heart of a woman in trouble" (Jer. 49:22).

If thou soar as an eagle, and though thou make thy nest among the stars, I will bring thee down from thence, saith the LORD (v.4).

The Lord warned them that even if they thought of themselves as being a highly exalted nation, like an eagle soaring up and setting its nest among the stars; He could bring them down. We learn in this that God is perfectly sovereign. He is above the nations. Everything that happens in every country is because He has so determined, whether we like it or not. He exalts nations; He humbles nations. This should make us able to trust Him no matter what is going on around us. "The Most High ruleth the kingdom of men, and giveth it to whomsoever He will, and setteth up over it the basest of men" (Dn. 4:17).

Our God humbles the wicked. This should make us as His people long to be humble. If we do not humble ourselves, He will humble us. Jesus said, "He who exalts himself will be humbled, and he who humbles himself will be exalted" (Matt. 23:12). Solomon counseled, "When pride comes, there comes also dishonor" (Prov. 11:2). The call of the prophet Micah is clear. "O man, He has declared to you what is good, and what the LORD requires of you: only to do justice, and to love mercy, and to humble yourself before your God" (Mic. 6:8). The Spirit instructs us through Paul, "Put on therefore, as the elect of God, holy and beloved, tender mercies, kindness, humility, meekness, gentleness, longsuffering" (Col. 3:12).

The trials of life are sometimes allowed by God to humble us so that we may find that He is our highest good (Ps. 16:2). He wants all our devotion, all our service, all our worship. He sees that there are constantly idols in our hearts. Our idols are all those things we love more than the Lord. They can be hobbies, friendships, work, business, family, our own self. God does whatever He has to do to remove those idols from us through afflictions so that He has the whole of our being.

2. The destruction of Edom (v.5-9)

If thieves came to you, or robbers by night (how you have been destroyed!), would they not steal what was enough for them? If grape-gatherers came to you, would they not leave some gleaning behind? (v.5)

The Edomites had prospered. Petra, the capital of Edom, was the center of Assyrian and Arabian trade. They were situated at a crossroads on The Kings' Highway or also called The Spice Road. At their location caravans made a stopover when traveling between Egypt and Mesopotamia, Syria and the Philistines to the north. They were within 1 km of two passes. God forewarned them here that they would lose all their wealth acquired through trade.

God reminded them about how thieves, robbers and grape pickers might have caused them to suffer certain losses, but the mountainous region where they lived meant that they could not do them as much harm. They could not rob them as they would have liked. They would steal something, but they could not take everything. Perhaps they had not been able to, but God would.

In Jeremiah 49:9 we read something very similar to what Obadiah the prophet wrote. "If grape gatherers had come against you, would they not have left gleanings? If thieves in the night, would they not have taken what was enough for them?" The grape pickers were those who gathered the grapes as they were harvested. The day would come when they would lose everything.

———◆———

How the things of Esau were searched! His hidden treasures were searched for (v.6)

Here the nation of Edom is identified as being Esau, because that was the name of their father. The same occurs in verses 8, 9, 18, 21. Esau's descendants also bore his name because they continued to manifest their sinful tendencies.

The prophet describes how the goods of Esau's sons had been rummaged through and their hidden treasures had been discovered. The Lord God had worked to expose the Edomites to their enemies and thus weaken them.

One of the things we learn from Edom is the fact that we should not give priority to the material, but that we should always give the greatest importance to what is spiritual. Edom had set its sights and affections on the transient, temporary and transitory. The Lord Jesus exhorts us concerning this. "Lay not up for yourselves treasures upon earth, where moth and rust doth corrupt, and where thieves break through and steal: but lay up for yourselves treasures in heaven, where neither moth nor rust doth corrupt, and where thieves do not break through nor steal. For where your treasure is, there your heart will be also" (Mt. 6:19-21). The apostle Paul also makes an appeal regarding this subject. "If then you have been raised with Christ, seek the things that are above, where Christ is, seated at the right hand of God. Set your minds on things above, not on things on earth" (Col. 3:1, 2).

All your allies have deceived you; they have brought you to the ends; those who were at peace with you have prevailed against you; those who ate your bread have laid a snare under you; there is no understanding in it (v.7).

God anticipates here that the destruction of Edom would come by the hand of their own allies. Nations like Ammon and Moab would have been involved in this treachery. They were to be destroyed by those with whom they had made an alliance or confederacy.

Let us note God's infinite wisdom: He confounds the nations that are at enmity with Israel in order to destroy them and to protect His people. This is something we also notice continually in the Psalms in David's experience. God is so wise that He works sovereignly so that those who are causing us great evils, are divided, confused and do not do to us what they had planned to do against us.

Edom would be destroyed by those who had been at peace with them. They would now deceive them and prevail against them. They would suffer themselves to be betrayed by being snared or ensnared. Their supposed friends and allies, those who ate bread with them because they benefited from their abundance, would be the ones who would end up hurting them . The description of the betrayal suffered by Edom resembles the worst betrayal mentioned in the Scriptures. David's prophecy of Judas Iscariot's betrayal of the Lord Jesus reads as follows, "Even the man of my peace, in whom I trusted, he that did eat of my bread, lifted up his heel against me" (Ps. 41:9). Eating bread with someone describes the closeness and communion enjoyed with someone, until that same person betrays him.

———————⬤———————

Shall I not cause to perish in that day, saith the LORD, the wise men of Edom, and the prudence of the mountain of Esau? (v.8)

Edom's destruction would come from God by allowing their goods to be exposed to their enemies (v.5, 6); their allies would betray them (v.7); and because God would confound their wise men (v.8, 9).

Edom had the reputation of having wise men. Their geographical location allowed them to acquire knowledge of the various countries that surrounded them and traveled through their territory. Now God assures them that He will destroy the wise men and the very wisdom that dwelt on Esau's mountain.

The same was anticipated by the prophet Jeremiah. "Concerning Edom. Thus saith the LORD of hosts, Is there no more wisdom in Teman? is counsel gone out of the wise? is their wisdom corrupt?" (Jer. 49:7). The psalmist also describes the fall of the wise. "For they shall see that even the wise die; that they perish in the same way as the foolish and the foolish, and leave their riches to others" (Ps. 49:10). Paul quoted the prophet Isaiah in writing to the Corinthians. "I will destroy the wisdom of the wise, and will destroy the understanding of the prudent" (1 Cor. 1:19). In detailing Job about the power and wisdom of God, he said: "He maketh counselors to walk void of counsel, and judges to be dumb" (Job 12:17). These passages are clear evidence that God glorifies himself by stripping the wise of their prudence by being infinitely superior to them. He warns those who boast in their wisdom. "Let not the wise man boast in his wisdom, nor let the brave man boast in his courage, nor let the rich man boast in his riches. But let him that shall glory in this, that he shall glory in this, that he understandeth and knoweth me, that I am the LORD, which sheweth lovingkindness, judgment, and righteousness in the earth: for these things will I, saith the LORD" (Jer. 9:23, 24).

Here we see again how God confounds the wicked in their machinations to protect those He loves in His heart. We should not fear those who harm us, even if they are strong, powerful and wicked. Ideally, the slandered and attacked Christian should not defend himself, but fear God who knows everything. He is the God who knows perfectly our situation and who knows how to confound our aggressors.

⟢ ● ⟣

And thy mighty men, O Teman, shall be dismayed; for every man shall be cut off from the mountain of Esau for the destruction (v.9).

Their wise men would be destroyed, but now Jehovah warns them that the mighty men were going to be frightened, frightened and broken. The devastation on Esau's mountain would be such that they would all be cut down by ravage. They would suffer a terrible slaughter.

Esau's mountain is Mount Seir of which we commonly read in Scripture (Gen. 32:3; 36:8, 9; Deut. 2:4, 5; Josh. 24:4; Ezek. 35:15).

Teman is mentioned. Esau's grandson was so named (Gen. 36:11). It became the name of a city in Esau's territory by being named after Esau's grandson. It was north of Edom and was where Eliphaz, Job's antagonist, was born (Job 4:1).

God's wisdom is seen in how he will destroy Edom. Being well hidden they were to be found and taken away (v.5, 6). They would be deceived by their allies (v.7). The wise among them would be made fools (v.8, 9). The brave would be intimidated and many would die by havoc or desolation (v.9).

God does not need swords and spears to defeat the wicked. God's power is accentuated by the fact that He often defeats His enemies without attacking them and allows them to self-destruct.

Obadiah is not the only one of the prophets to anticipate the fall of Edom. Isaiah prophesied that they will one day serve the nation of Israel (Isa. 11:14); for they will suffer the devastation of the drunken sword of the Lord of hosts (Isa. 34:5-17) and He will tread them down in His wrath (Isa. 63:1-3). The prophet Ezekiel anticipated that the time would come when God would cut off from Edom the men and their beasts to leave them desolate (Ezek. 35:1-15). The prophet Jeremiah announced: "Rejoice and be glad, O daughter of Edom, that dwellest in the land of Uz; even unto thee shall the cup come; thou shalt be drunken, and shalt vomit. Thy punishment is fulfilled, O daughter of Zion; he will no more cause thee to be led captive. He shall punish thine iniquity, O daughter of Edom; he shall uncover thy sins" (Lam. 4:21, 22). In Jeremiah 25:17-26 we find Edom in the list of those peoples who suffered the terrible wrath of God to fall upon them to destroy them. The prophet Malachi pronounced the following sentence upon them, "They shall build, and I will destroy; and they shall call them a land of wickedness, and a people against whom the LORD hath indignation for ever" (Mal. 1:4).

3. The sins of Edom (v.10-14)

For the injury to thy brother Jacob shame shall cover thee, and thou shalt be cut off forever (v.10).

Jehovah now reveals the sins of Edom. He does this because He is a righteous and just God. Not only does He punish sin, but also in His transparency, He shows people how and why He will punish them. God not only shows sinners the sin they have committed, but also informs them of the judgment they will suffer for their perversion.

We also read of the perversion of this nation in Amos 1:11, "Thus saith the LORD; For three sins of Edom, and for the fourth, I will not revoke his punishment; because he hath persecuted his brother with the sword, and hath violated all natural affection; and in his wrath he hath robbed him continually, and hath perpetually held a grudge."

The first sin he points out to them is their injury or violence against their brother Jacob, referring to the nation of Israel. The word reviling carries the idea of something being done against someone in an unjust or cruel way. It is possible that in part this refers to what we read in 2 Chronicles 28:17 - the Edomites attacked Israel and took some into captivity.

The fact that it was violence inflicted against his brother makes it even more serious and reprehensible before God. For the Lord all sins are repugnant in His sight, but here we learn how much He dislikes it when He sees conflict within a family. We might see this as referring to something like when we sin against a relative in the flesh or a brother in the Lord's family. It should greatly grieve God when He sees brothers in the flesh or spiritual brothers attacking each other. To avoid having this evil disposition toward others, we must obey what the Bible prescribes concerning this. "A new commandment I give unto you, that ye love one another; that as I have loved you, even so ye also love one another" (Jn. 13:34). Paul commands: "Be affectionate to one another with brotherly love" (Rom. 12:10). The apostle John points out: "If anyone says, 'I love God,' but hates his brother, he is a liar. For he who does not love his brother whom he has seen cannot love God whom he has not seen" (1 Jn. 4:20).

Because the Edomites had sinned against the Israelites, they would be covered with shame and cut off forever. God would humiliate them in various ways by covering them with shame, until they suffered the worst humiliation of all - death. Micah also speaks of Israel's enemies being covered with shame. God forces the sinner to suffer the humiliation he should feel for the sin he has committed. On their own initiative, they do not feel it because of their great indifference to God's holiness but the day comes when they are forced by the Lord Himself to do so.

Someone being cut off infers a person being killed. In this context, God was going to exterminate the Edomites for treating the Israelites the way they did. This would be to fulfill what was promised to Abraham. "I will bless those who bless you, and those who curse you I will curse" (Gen. 12:3). The prophet Isaiah also prophesied concerning the fall of Edom: "My sword shall be drunken in the heavens; behold, it shall come down upon

Edom in judgment, and upon the people of my curse. The sword of the LORD is full of blood, it is greased with fat, with the blood of lambs and goats, with the fat of the kidneys of rams: for the LORD hath sacrifices in Bozrah, and great slaughter in the land of Edom. And buffaloes shall fall with them, and bulls with calves; and their land shall be drunken with blood, and their dust shall be greased with fatness (Isa. 34:4-7).

In Ezekiel 25:12-14 we read concerning the punishment of Edom, "Thus saith the Lord GOD; Because of that which Edom hath done, in taking vengeance on the house of Judah, because they have dealt very treacherously, and have taken vengeance on them: therefore thus saith the Lord GOD; I will stretch out mine hand also upon Edom, and will cut off man and beast from it, and will make it desolate; from Teman even unto Dedan shall they fall by the sword. And I will lay my vengeance upon Edom in the hand of my people Israel, and they shall do in Edom according to mine anger and according to my wrath; and they shall know my vengeance, saith the Lord GOD." The prophet Joel also comments: "Edom shall become a desolate wilderness, because of the injury done to the children of Judah; for they have shed innocent blood in their land" (Joel 3:19).

<hr>

In the day when thou stoodest before them, when strangers carried away captive their host, and strangers entered into their gates, and cast lots for Jerusalem, thou also wast as one of them (v.11).

The second sin that is pointed out to them is the fact that Edom did nothing when strange enemies took the army of Israel into captivity. They did nothing to support Jacob when their enemies came through their gates and cast lots upon the city of Jerusalem. Not only did they sin because they did nothing, but they also committed wickedness because they participated in the harm that Israel suffered. Their failure to help made them accomplices and made them look like one of them.

Sometimes we think that by not doing something about certain cases we are pious and spiritual. There are difficult situations that arise, and instead of applying the Word of God, we decide to do nothing. Edom sinned greatly by not doing anything on behalf of Israel, but how many times this same sin is committed among believers who belong to the body of Jesus Christ? Many times we quote Numbers 32:23, "know that your sin will overtake you" when we want to warn someone that their sin will soon be discovered. These words God spoke to the Israelites when He warned them that they would be sinning and would have to suffer greatly for not doing anything about the enemies who were in the Promised Land. Let us not think that whenever we do not do something about something it is because we are holy and righteous. Many confuse things and think that they can exempt themselves from their responsibility because they are praying and waiting on the Lord . Many times we sin against God when we do nothing about a brother's situation that is complicated or controversial. God repudiates our being lukewarm as was the church in Laodicea (Rev. 3:15, 16). In 2 Corinthians Paul exhorted the church in Corinth to resolve the case of the brother who had sinned by taking his father's wife as his wife.

When it says that they cast lots over Jerusalem, it refers to the fact that Israel's enemies were dividing the spoils and plunder. In Joel 3:3 it says: "They cast lots for my people". The prophet

Nahum also commented on this. "She was carried away into captivity; her little ones also were dashed in the crossroads of every street, and upon her males they cast lots, and all her great ones were imprisoned with fetters" (Nah. 3:10). It clearly shows the wickedness of Edom because they did not participate in defending their brothers, but they did participate in taking the spoils that had belonged to them. This also shows the perversion of Israel for having suffered all this because of their constant disobedience to God. God continually works so that His perfect justice is always satisfied, even if it is in ways we do not understand.

For thou shouldest not have looked on in the day of thy brother, in the day of his calamity; thou shouldest not have rejoiced over the children of Judah in the day when they were lost, neither shouldest thou have boasted in the day of trouble (v.12).

Jehovah now condemns Edom for only looking at his brother without doing anything in the day of his misfortune. The word woe has to do with a calamity or disaster. The people of Idumea did nothing when Israel suffered greatly.

The picture drawn here is one of utterly cold and ruthless lack of restraint in Edom's cruel treatment of God's people. Edom showed no mercy and not a shred of compassion toward his brother Jacob. Perhaps this betrayed family relationship was one of the reasons why his "misfortune" was so final.

What are we doing about the disaster and calamity that some are suffering? Are we like Abraham who risked his life to rescue his nephew Lot? Or are we like the Corinthians who abandoned a man who had repented of his sin? How many of us are like Cain, who in the face of our responsibility for our brothers, say to the Lord, "Am I my brother's keeper?"

God also condemned the sons of Esau for rejoicing over the destruction of Judah and for boasting in the day of their distress. This would result in their having to suffer the same at God's hand. They sowed indifference, mockery and boasting; and they would reap the same. Hence the admonition of the Holy Spirit. "Be not deceived; God cannot be mocked: for whatsoever a man soweth, that shall he also reap" (Gal. 6:7).

Through Edom's bad example, God is teaching us about His desire for us to show His grace to those who harm us. Not only should we look to our brothers when they suffer, but we should also help them in whatever way we can when the day of their misfortune comes upon them. In spite of the rivalry, the Lord God had commanded Israel to love those of Edom (Deut. 23:7), those who had caused them great evils. Neither should we rejoice or speak arrogantly when brothers who have wronged us fall. We should carefully and solemnly consider the warning of the wise Solomon. "When thine enemy falleth, rejoice not: and when thine enemy stumbleth, let not thine heart be glad; lest the LORD look upon him, and it displease him, and his wrath turn away from him" (Prov. 24:17, 18). As we continue to meditate on what Paul wrote in Galatians 6:7, let us think that if we want God to show mercy to us in the day of our distress, we must show mercy to others.

You should not have entered the gate of my people in the day of their calamity; no, you should not have looked on their evil in the day of their calamity, nor laid hold of their goods in the day of their calamity (v.13).

The Lord now condemns Edom for having entered the gate of Jerusalem in the day of her destruction, for having looked upon her evil in the day of her destruction, and for having laid hold of her goods in the day of her calamity.

They took advantage of their brother Jacob and betrayed them. God would later allow them to suffer the same. It is interesting to note that each of their sins were committed on the same day that Israel suffered calamity. We see here a clear demonstration of God's perfect justice.

We see again how it is that at the root of all sin is pride. Edom began to be arrogant, this led them to do nothing about the trouble Israel suffered, they rejoiced over what happened to them and ended up stealing their goods. The Christian must always remember the imperative need daily to put to death the sins that are in one. Paul instructs, "Put to death therefore what is earthly in you: fornication, impurity, inordinate passions, evil desires, and covetousness, which is idolatry" (Col. 3:5). If we do not put sin to death, as happened with Edom, one wickedness will lead us to commit another wickedness, and this will lead us to suffer the consequences of our folly. The 17th century Puritan John Owen wisely said: "Kill sin or sin will kill you". We must do something promptly about the sin in us, otherwise we will suffer the consequences. "Each one is tempted, when from his own concupiscence he is drawn away and enticed. Then when lust hath conceived, it bringeth forth sin: and sin, when it is finished, bringeth forth death" (Jas. 1:14, 15).

———◉———

Neither should you have stood at the crossroads to kill those who escaped from them; nor should you have delivered up those who remained in the day of trouble (v.14).

Sadly, the Edomites stood at the crossroads to murder the Israelites who tried to escape the terrible danger they were suffering at the hands of their enemies. They also arrested those who remained in Jerusalem on that sad day of Israel's distress. Woe to those in the church of Christ Jesus whose disloyalty leads them to reproach, betray, and do away with their own brethren!

Everything that happened to the people of Idumea shows that the Lord severely punishes those who wrong those who cannot defend themselves. The sin committed by Edom against Israel was committed against God. "He will judge the afflicted of the people, He will save the children of the needy, and crush the oppressor" (Ps. 72:4). He that oppresseth the poor to increase his gain, or that giveth to the rich, shall surely be made poor" (Prov. 22:16).

4. The omen of Edom (v.15, 16)

For the day of the LORD is near upon all nations; as thou hast done, so shall it be done unto thee; thy reward shall be upon thy head (v.15).

The day of the LORD makes us think of His anger and of Him punishing the wicked. God warned Esau of the wrath they would suffer for their sinful attitudes and wicked actions they inflicted upon His people. They would be judged on the basis of what they had done to others. Their recompense, that is, their treatment of others, would be returned upon their own heads. They would suffer for every one of their perversions committed.

In considering the day of Jehovah, it would be helpful to consider other days mentioned in the Scriptures in order to place ourselves accurately in God's prophetic program.

1. Day of salvation (2 Cor. 6:2). It began on the day of Pentecost and will end with the rapture of the church.

2. Day of Christ, Jesus Christ or the Lord Jesus (1 Cor. 1:8). Includes: Rapture of the Church, the Judgment Seat of Christ and the Marriage of the Lamb.

3. Day of the Lord. Includes: The Tribulation, the Coming in glory of the Lord and the Millennium. Passages that focus on this day: Isa. 13:6, 9; Ezek. 13:5; 30:3; Joel 1:15; 2:11, 31; 3:14; Am. 5:18; Zeph. 1:7; Zech. 14:1; Mal. 4:5; Acts 2:20; 1 Thess. 5:2; 2 Pet. 3:10.

4. Day of Jehovah's wrath (Zeph. 1:18; 2:2). Includes: the Second Half of the Tribulation.

5. Day of Judgment (2 Pet. 3:7). Includes: the Great White Throne Judgment.

6. Day of God (2 Pet. 3:12). Includes: Future Eternity.

We speak here of the foreshadowing of Edom in this section, because the day of Jehovah refers to the judgment on that nation, and is a foreshadowing of God's coming punishment on this world after Jesus comes to rapture the church. In the Old Testament it is very clear that the day of the Lord has a partial fulfillment and a final fulfillment. The wrath of the Lord that would fall on Edom, anticipates the terrible punishment that will fall on the inhabitants of the earth in a coming day. We see the same in other prophetic books such as Joel. The plague that would devastate Judah was a foreshadowing of what the land would suffer later. This double application of prophecy was applied by Peter in the sermon he gave in Jerusalem (Acts 2:16-21). This means that the final fulfillment of what was prophesied to Edom will be in the Great Tribulation. On some occasions, the day of the Lord is something of which Israel is warned, but in this case it is something of which a Gentile nation such as Edom is warned.

What Edom would suffer in the day of the Lord, which would be when they would suffer greatly, is a prelude to what the Lord will do to the earth in a day to come. The day of the Lord will result in the nations being deceived by the beast and suffering horrible misery for believing the lie and rejecting God. In Revelation we read of the judgments related to the horsemen, seals, trumpets, cup, the battle of Armageddon and the final judgments. As Obadiah said to Edom, all will receive on their heads the reward of which they were made worthy. We can find peace in the fact that God will punish all those who in one way or another wronged those who are His. We should also bless the name of God, for the church will not be on earth when all these portentous judgments take place.

———◦———

As ye have drunk upon my holy mountain, so shall all nations drink continually; they shall drink, and swallow down, and be as though they had not been (v.16).

God speaks to them about drinking because His wrath would be poured out on sinners as if they drank the cup of His wrath. In Jeremiah 49:12 we read, "For thus saith the LORD; Behold, they that were not condemned to drink the cup shall surely drink; and shalt thou be altogether acquitted? Thou shalt not be acquitted, but shalt surely drink." The cup is used in the Word of God to represent the Lord's punishment of the wicked (e.g., Jer. 25:15). The prophet Isaiah announced that the cup of God's wrath would be taken from His people to be given to those who afflicted them. "Thus saith the LORD thy Lord, and thy God, which pleadeth for his people, Behold, I have taken out of thine hand the cup of stunnedness, the dregs of the cup of my wrath; thou shalt drink it no more. And I will put it into the hand of thine anguishers, who said to thy soul, Bow down, and we will pass over thee. And thou hast made thy body as the earth, and as a way, that they may pass over thee" (Isa. 51:22, 23).

The Lord took the cup of God's wrath on the cross, but those who do not believe in Him will have to take it themselves forever in the lake of fire by being smitten by God eternally and forever.

Chalice of death and curse filled for me, you took with resignation, drinking it for me,

and its bitterness turned your love into blessing for me.

In Revelation 14:10 we read about those who will suffer tribulation: "he shall drink of the wine of the wrath of God, which is poured out pure into the cup of His indignation; and he shall be tormented with fire and brimstone before the holy angels and before the Lamb".

Edom had drunk the wrath of God on the holy mountain of the Lord which is Zion or Jerusalem. They were to drink and swallow the cup of the Lord. To gulp down carries the idea that they would swallow it whole and completely. Edom was to suffer by the hand of God, but the same was to happen to the nations (v.15, 16). The day would come when they would drink God's judgment in full. "For the cup is in the hand of the LORD, and the wine is fermented, full of mingled wine; and He poureth out of the same; they shall drink it to the full, and all the wicked of the earth shall drink it" (Ps. 75:8). The day will come when the nations will experience God's chastisement continually, they will swallow it up and it will be so devastating to them that they will become as if they had not been. Our God is Jealous. He protects those whom He loves and He annihilates those who sin against Him.

5. Edom's rival (v.17-21)

But on Mount Zion there shall be a remnant that shall be saved; and it shall be holy, and the house of Jacob shall recover its possessions (v.17).

In this last section of the prophecy, the Lord lets Edom know what He will do with Israel, their rivals whom they hated so much. Eager to break them, He first revealed to them that He would destroy them (v.16) and now He communicates to them about the exaltation of the people whom He loved so much.

God affirms that not only would there be judgment on Mount Zion, but that on that same mountain, He would also bless His people and He would do so in three ways.

The three blessings are:

---

1. He will rescue or save them. No one can besiege or destroy them. Spiritually, they will also be saved. A remnant of Israel will be converted to God. What the apostle Paul anticipated will be fulfilled. "All Israel shall be saved" (Rom. 11:26).

2. There will be holiness. This is something that will characterize the future reign of Christ. Sin predominates in this world at present; but holiness will characterize the world in the future under the reign of the Messiah.

3. The house of Jacob will rejoice in obtaining possessions. The nation that was stripped of all its possessions will recover

all its possessions and enjoy immense wealth because of God's mercy.

These three blessings of God for Israel mentioned here will be fulfilled on the day of the Lord in the future reign of our King. From Mount Zion, Jesus the King of glory will reign.

This is one of many texts that should cause us to reject what is called the replacement or fulfillment theory which teaches that God has rejected Israel forever and that He has no future purpose for His people. It teaches that the promises made to Israel will be fulfilled in the church. The church has not replaced Israel. God very clearly teaches in His Word that He still has wonderful purposes with Israel for when His Son comes the second time.

God's faithfulness will result in Him fulfilling the promises He has made to His people. He cannot break His promises. The writer to the Hebrews states something that is most comforting to His people. "Wherefore God, willing more abundantly to shew unto the heirs of promise the immutability of His counsel, hath sworn by an oath: that by two immutable things, wherein it is impossible for God to lie, we might have the strongest consolation, which we have come to lay hold on the hope of hope

set before us" (Heb. 6:17, 18).

⸺⚬⸺

The house of Jacob shall be a fire, and the house of Joseph shall be a flame, and the house of Esau shall be stubble, and they shall burn them, and consume them: there shall not be left of the house of Esau; for the LORD hath spoken it (v.18).

Now Israel is presented as being at the center of God's plans for dealing with the nations of the world by punishing the transgressors. The house of Jacob will be as a fire and the house of Joseph will be a flame. God's justice will be partly executed through Israel. Jacob refers to the southern kingdom and Joseph to the northern kingdom (it is common in Scripture that when speaking of the northern kingdom, it is referred to as Ephraim, Joseph's youngest son). How wonderful it is that a nation that had remained divided, we now find united (Ezek. 37:15-23).

In Zechariah 12:2, 6 it says: "Behold, I will make Jerusalem a cup that shall shake all the peoples round about against Judah, in the siege against Jerusalem... In that day I will make the captains of Judah as a brazier of fire among the wood, and as a burning torch among the sheaves; and they shall devour all the peoples round about on the right hand and on the left; and Jerusalem shall be inhabited again in her place, in Jerusalem". This means that Israel will be used as an instrument by God to be His cup of chastisement, that through them righteous judgment will be imparted to the nations.

Esau shall be as stubble that is easily burned. The word stubble in Hebrew can also mean: "stubble" and "chaff". The fire of God's righteousness will consume and devour those of Idumea. They thought they could remain forever, but as has been the case with many nations, God has destroyed them and made them disappear. In Jeremiah 49, the destruction of Edom is compared to the destruction of Sodom and Gomorrah. God warns Edom that there will be none left of the house of Esau. They will be completely wiped out.

God is reversing things. All that Edom enjoyed and all that Israel had suffered in the past will be reversed in a coming day.

Edom will suffer and Israel will enjoy God's blessings. How can we be sure that a powerful nation like Edom would be exterminated? Because the Lord had said so, says the prophet Obadiah.

------◦------

And those of the Negev shall possess the mountain of Esau, and those of the Sephelah shall possess the Philistines; they shall also possess the fields of Ephraim, and the fields of Samaria; and Benjamin shall possess Gilead (v.19).

The Lord also promises Israel that they will possess several territories that were theirs, but which they had lost because of their rebellion against Him.

They would possess the Mount of Esau; those of the Sephelah or valley of the Philistines, the fields of Ephraim; the fields of Samaria; and Benjamin to Gilead.

In a coming day, Israel will possess all the territory that it should always have enjoyed under its possession. In every direction, the Hebrews will inherit the land that had always been theirs. They will possess territory to the south by taking possession of the Negev. They will possess territory on the coast by taking possession of the valley of the Philistines on the west. They will possess territory in the central part by taking possession of Ephraim and Samaria. They will possess territory east of the Jordan River by taking possession of Gilead.

The promise made to Abraham will be fulfilled. "Thy seed shall be as the dust of the earth, and thou shalt spread abroad to the west, and to the east, and to the north, and to the south" (Gen. 28:14). All that God promised Abraham, Isaac and Jacob, concerning the land He would give to their descendants, has been fulfilled and will be fulfilled forever.

———◉———

And the captives of this army of the children of Israel shall possess that which the Canaanites possessed as far as Zarephath; and the captives of Jerusalem which are in Sepharad shall possess the cities of the south (v.20).

It is prophesied here that the captives would also possess the land of the Canaanites and the cities of the south. It was partly fulfilled when the exiles returned to their land, but it will be completely fulfilled in the reign of Christ when Israel possesses the land. The nation that was in captivity will enjoy dominion and greatness in a coming day.

Zarephath was a coastal city located south of Sidon (1 Kings 17:9). Sepharad was a city to which the Israelites were taken in exile. Its location is unknown. This is its only mention in the entire Bible.

With what is prophesied in verses 19 and 20, the importance of the Israelites' territory in relation to God's covenant made with Abraham is once again confirmed. All that God promised to the father of faith will be completely fulfilled. Our faith is strengthened by seeing that God fulfills everything he promises.

———◉———

And saviors shall go up to Mount Zion to judge the mountain of Esau; and the kingdom shall be the Lord's (v.21).

The final promise of God is that saviors will go to Mount Zion to judge the mountain of Esau and in that way the kingdom will be Jehovah's.

Esau would have no one to rescue them, but Israel would have those who would deliver them on behalf of God, the great Rescuer. The word rescuers can also be translated as "deliverers" or "rescuers". They are those whom God will choose "to judge the mountain of Esau". They will execute the wrath of God upon the children of Esau to devastate them according to His perfect justice.

Commentator Arno C. Gaebelein comments on another aspect of the rescuers:

> chosen ones who go forth to teach all nations and to make known the glory of the King among them. For "the kingdom shall be the Lord's".

Obadiah ends by consoling Israel, assuring them that the kingdom will belong to the Lord. At the end of it all, after Satan tried to rule the world, after man thought he could establish mighty nations, "the kingdom shall be the Lord's". We read about this very thing in Psalm 22:28, "The kingdom is the Lord's, and He shall rule the nations". When Isaiah writes about the kingdom of Jesus, he declares that the Lord will be "a crown of glory in the hand of the LORD, and a diadem of a kingdom in the hand of thy God" (Isa. 62:3).

The day will come when the kingdom of God will have as its center Mount Zion or the glorious city of Jerusalem. In Psalm 2 we read what God says about His Son, "I have set my king upon Zion, my holy mountain". The Lord God anticipates that He will work for His Son Jesus Christ to reign over the whole earth from the holy city. This is a fact that no one can prevent its fulfillment, no matter who opposes it. Revelation 11:15 confirms that during the tribulation: "And the seventh angel sounded, and there were great voices in heaven, saying, The kingdoms of the world are become the kingdoms of our Lord, and of his Christ; and he shall reign for ever and ever.

The climax of the prophecy is found in the final statement: "the kingdom shall be Jehovah's". In spite of the opposition, the fury and the intrigues of the nations, God has set His King, the Lord Jesus Christ, His beloved Son, upon the throne (Ps. 2). He will be the supreme Ruler, the King of kings and Lord of lords (Rev. 19:16). He is Jehovah and will reign universally, without rival or dispute: "And Jehovah shall be king over all the earth: in that day there shall be one Lord, and one name shall be his name" (Zechariah 14:9).

Conclusion

Obadiah's prophecy is clear, concise and undeniable. God will reign on earth. Jesus will be King of kings and Lord of lords. God is the King of Israel (Isa. 44:6). Not only is He the King of Israel, but He is also the "God of all kingdoms" (Isa. 37:16). Not only is He the God of all kingdoms, but He is also the "King of kings" (1 Tim. 6:15). Not only is He the King of kings, but He is also the "great King over all the earth" (Ps. 47:2). Not only is He the King over all the earth, but He is also the "King of the ages" (1 Tim. 1:17). God is our King (Ps. 47:6). All this agrees with what Obadiah prophesied. The Lord is the King who rules at present over all things and the day is coming when "the kingdom shall be the Lord's".

In an invisible way, "the kingdom of God is at hand" (Mark 1:15). To that kingdom belong all of us who have placed ourselves under Christ's authority through repentance and faith in Him (Col. 1:13). We say that this is invisible because it cannot yet be fully seen. But the day is coming when the Lord's kingdom will be fully visible, for we will see it in all its splendor and in all its glory.

Our hearts should respond favorably in different ways to such a magnificent promise concerning the Lord's kingdom. We should give Him all that we are, for the kingdom is His. We should trust in Him with all our hearts, for the kingdom is His. We must mourn over the evils of this world, but not allow it to discourage or distract us. Let us spread the King's message. Let us represent our King well. History is already written, and when it all comes to an end, we know that we will triumph because our King has conquered. Our King is victorious. His kingdom cannot be moved (Heb. 12:28) and His kingdom is eternal (2 Pet. 1:11).

Don't miss out!

Visit the website below and you can sign up to receive emails whenever Bible Sermons publishes a new book. There's no charge and no obligation.

https://books2read.com/r/B-A-MZBS-QENED

BOOKS 2 READ

Connecting independent readers to independent writers.

Also by Bible Sermons

A Collection of Biblical Sermons
The Power of Great Gospel Words
The Power of Prayer: Men Ought Always to Pray
The Power of the Single Life in Christ
Analyzing The Power of a Life in Christ

Bible Characters Collection
Analyzing Biblical Scenes: 62 Inspiring Christian Teachings
from the Old Testament

Notes in the New Testament
Analyzing Notes in the Book of Matthew: Fulfillments of Old
Testament Prophecies
Analyzing Notes in the Book of Mark: Finding Peace in
Difficult Times
Analyzing Notes in the Book of Luke: The Divine Love of Jesus
Revealed

Analyzing Notes in the Book of John: John's Contribution to the New Testament Scriptures

Analyzing Notes in the Book of the Acts of the Apostles: A Journey of Continuation in the Work of Jesus

Overflying The Bible

Symbols in the Bible: Healthy Christian Doctrine

Bible Introduction: Overflying The Bible from Genesis by Brethren in the Faith

Chronological Prophecy: Things That Will Happen on Earth

Bible Study: Genesis 1. Creation in Six Days

Teaching in the Bible class

Sunday School Lessons: 182 Bible Stories

Bible Class for Beginners: 50 Beautiful Lessons

Lessons for Sunday School: 62 Biblical Characters

How to Teach in Sunday School: A Guide for Bible Class Teachers

Teaching in the Bible Classroom

Studying Teaching in the Bible Classroom: A Teacher's Guide

The Education of Labor in the Bible

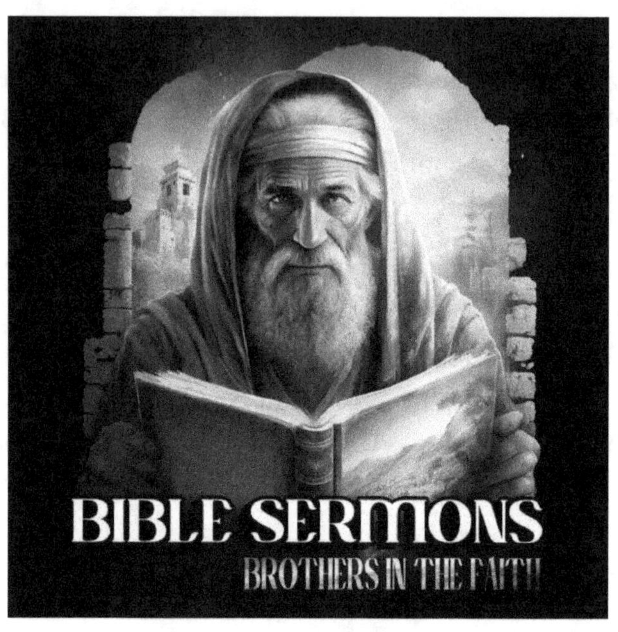

About the Author

This bible study series is perfect for Christians of any level, from children to youth to adults. It provides an engaging and interactive way to learn the Bible, with activities and discussion topics that will help deepen your understanding of scripture and strengthen your faith. Whether you're a beginner or an experienced Christian, this series will help you grow in your knowledge of the Bible and strengthen your relationship with God. Led by brothers with exemplary testimonies and extensive knowledge of scripture, who congregate in the name of the Lord Jesus Christ throughout the world.